ROLLER COASTER
DESIGN AND ENGINEERING

- Introduction to the Roller coasters
- What Are Roller Coasters?
- History of the Roller Coasters
- Russia's Ice Mountains
- France's Wheeled Coasters
- Making it Safe and Fun
- Roller Coaster Gets Better!
- Improving Designs
- Roller Coasters From Simple to Sensational!
- The World's Most Amazing Roller Coasters
- How Are Roller Coasters Built?
- Wooden Roller Coasters
- Steel Roller Coasters
- Hybrid Roller Coasters
- Types of Roller Coaster Rides
- Traditional Coasters
- Strata Coasters
- Flying Coasters
- Designing Roller Coasters
- Pre-Construction Planning
- Roller coaster layout
- Parts of the Roller coaster layout
- Loops, Turns, and Twists
- Corkscrews, figure-eight
- Hills and Drops Are Not Just for Fun
- No Engine Needed!
- The Mighty Lift Hill
- Lifts Systems
- Potential Energy
- Energy Transfer
- Kinetic Energy
- Understanding Momentum
- Engineering Calculations
- Weightlessness
- Zero-G Rolls
- Roller Coaster Dynamics
- Effect of Gravity
- Effect of Inertia
- Effect of Centrifugal force
- Designing Using Computers
- Installing the Support Structure
- Installing the Track
- Chairs' Comfort and Safety
- Testing Roller Coaster Design
- Sandbags Test
- Roller Coaster Test Runs
- Control Room Behind the Scenes
- Maintenance
- Engineering Updates

Just Scan and Explore!

Designing and Engineering of Roller Coasters for kids© 2024 All rights reserved. No part of this book may be reproduced or used in any manner without written permission of the copyright owner except for the use of quotations in a book review. For more information contact us, First paperback edition March 2024 Book.

ROLLER COASTER

Imagine the Thrill!

Imagine zooming along a track at lightning speed, with the wind whooshing past your face and your heart racing with excitement. That's the thrill of a roller coaster! These amazing rides are like giant, twisty puzzles made of steel and wood, designed to give us a safe and exhilarating adventure.

Welcome to the fun world of roller coasters!

What Are Roller Coasters?

Roller coasters are super fun rides found in amusement parks all over the world. They come in all shapes and sizes, with tall drops, sharp turns, and loop-the-loops that turn you upside down! But have you ever wondered how they started and what makes them so exciting?

Discover the Magic!

A roller coaster is like a train full of thrills, built with loops, drops, and high-speed turns! Unlike regular trains, roller coasters use gravity and special tracks to whoosh you around at exciting speeds, giving you an adrenaline rush like no other!

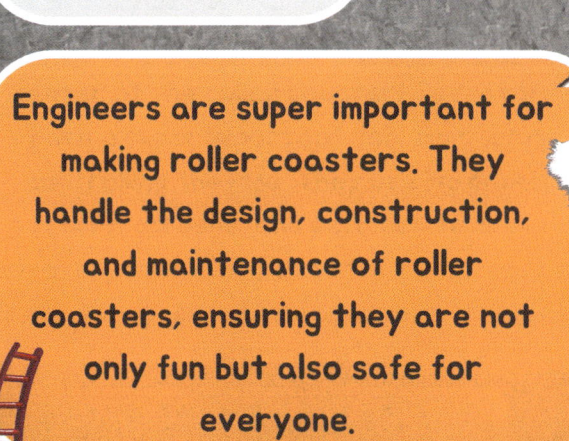

Engineers are super important for making roller coasters. They handle the design, construction, and maintenance of roller coasters, ensuring they are not only fun but also safe for everyone.

They are like the secret heroes who make roller coasters awesome! They use their smarts and creativity to make sure the rides are super fun and safe

HISTORY OF ROLLER COASTER

Russia's Ice Mountains

Are you ready to learn about the amazing history of roller coasters and how they've evolved over time?

They made exciting ice slides, like frosty adventure rides!

The story of roller coasters begins hundreds of years ago, not with fancy steel tracks, but with ice! Long ago, people in Russia created huge ice slides in winter. These were massive, sloping structures built in the winter. People would climb to the top of these slides and rush down them on sleds made of wood or blocks of ice, enjoying a thrilling ride.

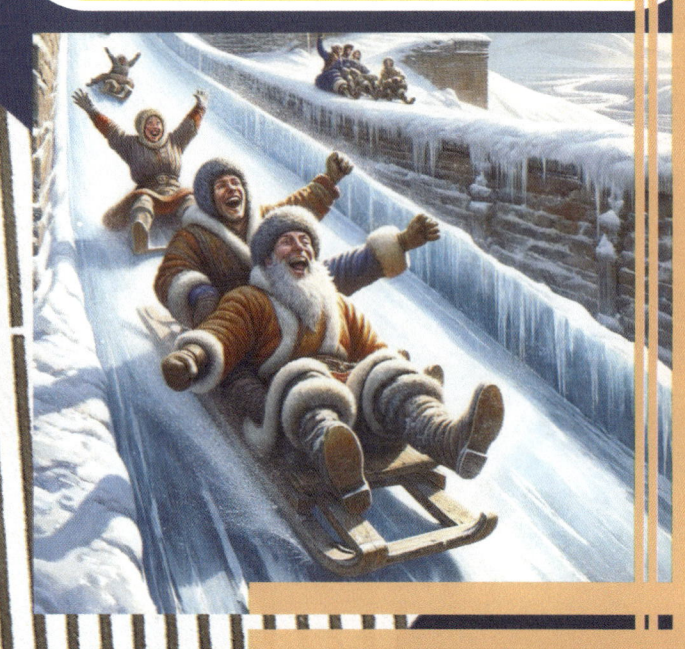

Imagine it's a long time ago in Russia, and it's winter. People there made huge slides out of ice, like giant frozen slides at a playground.

These slides were often coated with water to freeze over the ice, making them slicker and the ride down faster. The slides became so popular that they built more improved cart with wooden supports to make them steeper and taller, creating more thrilling rides.

FRANCE'S WHEELED COASTERS

Later the idea travelled from Russia to France. People in France were thinking about how to make sleds more fun. The French were especially creative. They figured out that if they put the sleds on tracks, the ride would be smoother and safer. This was the start of roller coasters!

GO!

They also started adding wheels to sleds and tracks to slides. People could sit in the cart and ride along the track, enjoying the exciting twists and turns.

LES MONTAGNES RUSSES À BELLEVILLE

Later in Paris, they created a fantastic roller coaster named "Les Montagnes Russes à Belleville,". Imagine a ride with special old cars that clung to the tracks, twisting and turning for an extra fun adventure.

FUN

WOW

HAVE FUN

MAKING IT SAFE AND FUN

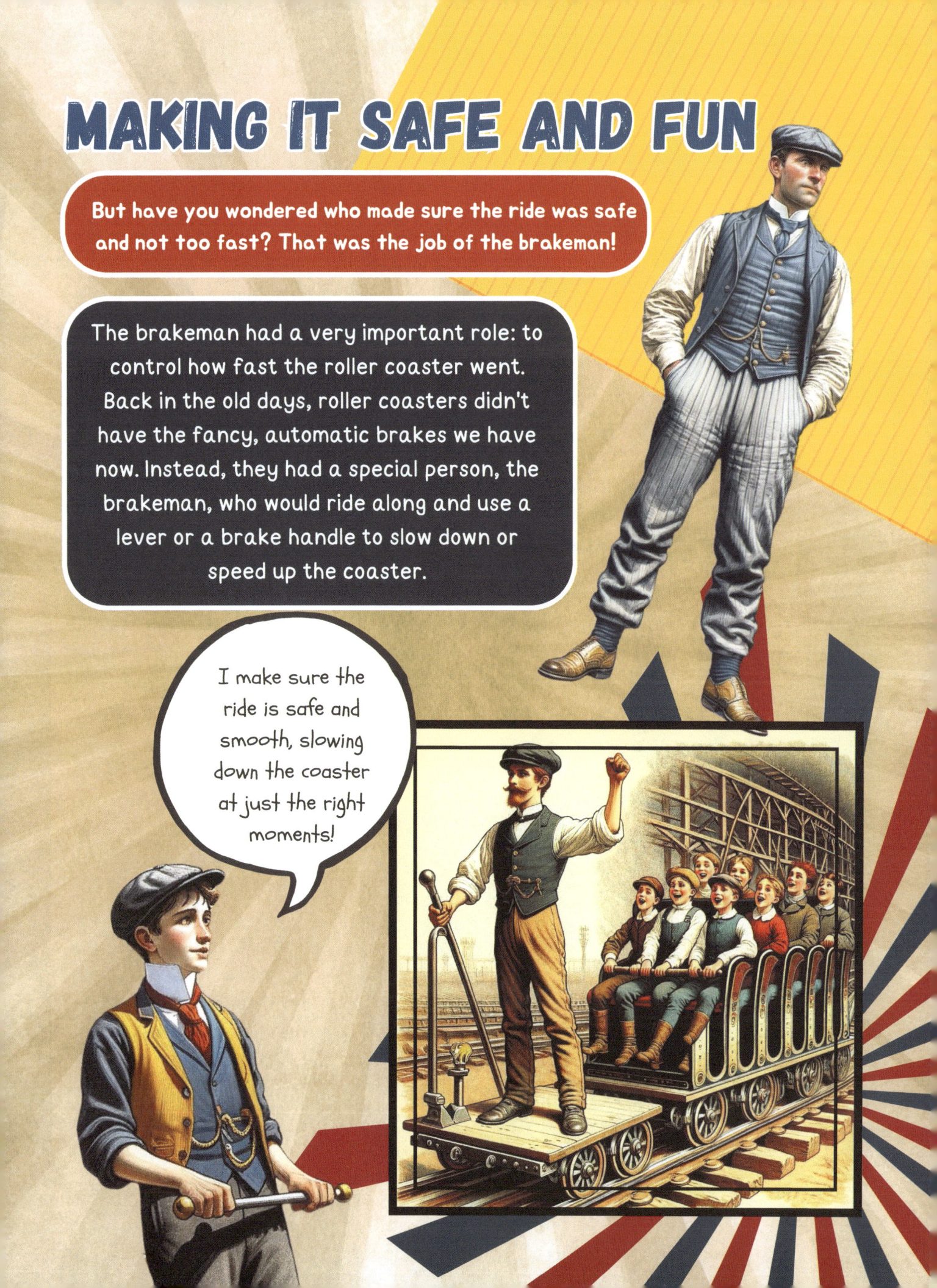

But have you wondered who made sure the ride was safe and not too fast? That was the job of the brakeman!

The brakeman had a very important role: to control how fast the roller coaster went. Back in the old days, roller coasters didn't have the fancy, automatic brakes we have now. Instead, they had a special person, the brakeman, who would ride along and use a lever or a brake handle to slow down or speed up the coaster.

I make sure the ride is safe and smooth, slowing down the coaster at just the right moments!

Roller Coaster Gets Better!

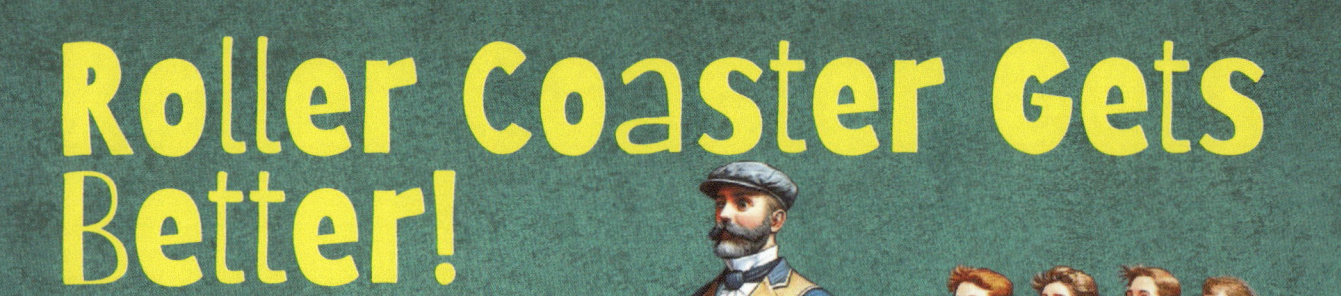

Back then, for safety, besides the brake men, they used simpler methods like making sure the tracks were smooth and the carts were well-built. They didn't have today's technology, so they relied on careful design and constant checks to keep everyone smiling and secure on the ride.

After the first roller coaster in Paris, things got really exciting in the world of roller coasters. People loved the twists and turns, and they wanted more. So, clever builders and engineers started to think "How can we make roller coasters even more fun?"

"I create fun roller coaster rides, making sure they're exciting and safe."

Taller TRACKS

First, they made the tracks taller, so the cars could zoom down faster and make everyone scream with joy. The higher the track, the faster the ride, and that meant more excitement! Leap-The-Dips is one of the first very tall wooden roller coasters located in Pennsylvania.

Stronger materials

Then, they used better materials to make the tracks stronger. This meant the roller coasters could have more loops and drops without anyone worrying about safety. Matterhorn Bobsleds, California, was the world's first tubular steel roller coaster.

IMPROVING DESIGNS

Comfy Seats

They also thought about comfort. Now, the seats were made to be more comfortable. It was common to have two or four seats per row, allowing for a shared ride experience.

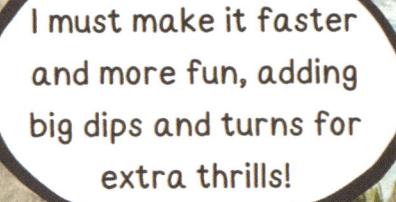

I must make it faster and more fun, adding big dips and turns for extra thrills!

Cool Themes

Roller coasters started to have themes, like pirates or space adventures. This made the rides not just fun but like a story, with each twist and turn feeling like a part of an exciting tale.

Safety first

They did not forget safety, so they added safety bars to make sure everyone stayed snug in their seats during the ride.

SAFETY FIRST

Smooth Rides

The rides became smoother, too. Engineers worked hard to make sure the roller coaster didn't jerk you around too much, so you could enjoy the speed without the bumps.

Amazing Tricks

Roller coasters started doing tricks that no one had seen before, like spinning around, or even going backwards!

Big Drops and Loops

And let's not forget the drops and loops! They became bigger and loopier, making everyone's stomach do funny flips and giving us all a bigger thrill.

ROLLER COASTERS
From Simple to Sensational!

Over the years, roller coasters have improved a lot. They went from simple carts on tracks to amazing rides that make our hearts race and our smiles stretch from ear to ear. This didn't just happen by chance; it took super smart engineers, creative designers, and safety specialists to dream up and build roller coasters that are not just rides, but incredible experiences.

There are so many different kinds of roller coasters, like a whole bunch of different ice cream flavors, each one with its own special fun!

Wow, our design is really delivering the thrills! Everything's running smoothly and safely.

OOooo!!

WOW

The World's Most Amazing
ROLLER COASTERS

The longest roller coaster is the Steel Dragon 2000 in Japan, stretching over 8,000 feet long!

The oldest operating roller coaster is Leap-the-Dips in Pennsylvania, USA. It's been thrilling riders since 1902!

Formula Rossa (UAE): Hold onto your hats! The fastest coaster on Earth, zooming at speeds of 149 mph!

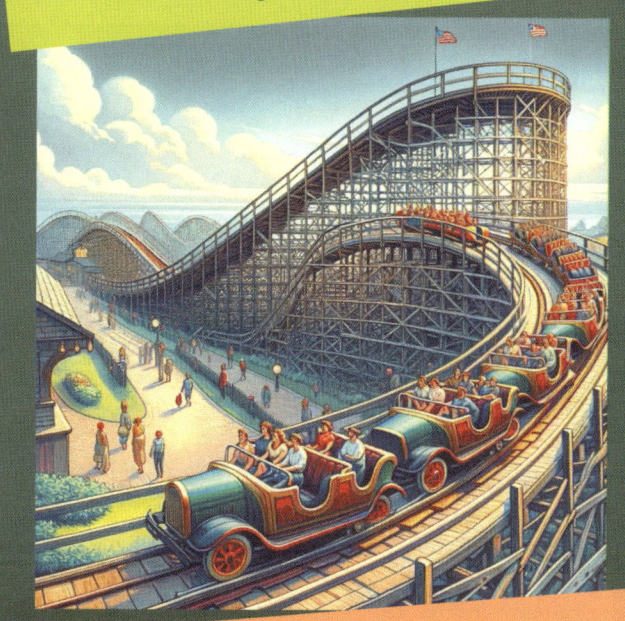

Kingda Ka (USA): The tallest coaster in the world! It shoots you up 456 feet into the sky!

HOW ARE ROLLER COASTERS BUILT?

Before engineers start building a roller coaster, they carefully plan and consider many important questions to decide on the best design for the ride.

Who is going to ride the coaster? Is the coaster for kids, families, or thrill-seekers?

What is the track layout? How the track will twist, turn, and loop to make the ride fun and memorable?

What materials will be best for this roller coaster? Should we use steel, wood, or a combination of both?

Are we following all the important safety rules in our design?

What is the type of cart? How many people it will hold and what safety features it will have?

What is the speed of the coaster?

What cool, new things can we add to make our roller coaster special and different?

Engineers use their imagination and creativity to come up with ideas for the roller coaster. They think about how tall it should be, how fast it should go, and how many twists and turns it will have.

How tall should the track be to provide the desired excitement and speed but still be safe?

How much space do we have for the roller coaster?

What is our budget for building the roller coaster?

How can we make the best ride possible within this budget?

What speed do we want the roller coaster to reach?

How much noise will the roller coaster make, and could this affect nearby areas or communities?

How do we ensure that the ride is comfortable as well as thrilling?

CHOOSING Materials

When engineers start planning a roller coaster, the first big decision is what to make it out of. They can choose wood, steel, or even a mix of both!

Wooden Roller Coasters

These are the old-school kind, made mostly of wood. They give a bumpy, exciting ride and make a lot of noise as the train goes over the tracks. They look really classic, like the roller coasters your grandparents might have ridden!

engineers still build wooden roller coasters today. They are special because they have a classic feel and many people still enjoy the old-fashioned wooden coasters because they're exciting in their own way.

AHHH! WOO HOO!

The wooden coaster's noise? It's cool! Sounds like the coaster's roaring to life, hyping us up for the wild ride ahead!

Steel Roller Coasters

These are made from strong metal and can be built much taller, faster, and with loops and twists that wooden coasters can't do. They give a smoother ride than wooden ones and can do all sorts of wild, fun shapes.

Hybrid Roller Coasters

These mix wood and steel, taking the best parts of both. They might have the wooden structure's classic look and feel but use steel tracks to allow for upside-down loops and steeper drops.

TYPES OF ROLLER COASTER RIDES

Once they've picked the material, engineers decide what kind of ride they want to create. There are many different types of coaster rids. Each type offers a different fun experience!

TRADITIONAL COASTERS

They are kind of like old pirate ships on rails!

These are the classic ones made of wood, where the track is flat, and the ride is bumpy and thrilling, filled with sharp turns and quick drops. They have a special rumbly feel and make clackety-clack sounds as they race along the track, going up, down, and around in fun ways. People love them because they feel a bit wild and give you a sense of riding something historic and thrilling

STEEL COASTER

This type of roller coaster is known for its crazy flips, twists, and the ability to turn riders upside down. These coasters provide thrilling experiences of being turned head over heels.

People love them because they give super smooth rides, can do awesome loops and twists, and make you feel like you're flying on a thrilling adventure. It's like riding a rocket ship that twists, turns, and dives, giving you a fun rush every time!

Steel roller coasters let us build really tall and twisty rides that are super fun!

Wooohoooo!

STRATA COASTERS

Strata coasters are super tall roller coasters that reach up into the sky! They are like giant towers of fun, because they are at least 400 feet tall—that's taller than most buildings!

Strata coasters are like sky-touching rocket rides, zooming you way up high, where the clouds wave hello!

People love them because they go really, really high and then zoom down super fast, making the ride super exciting and giving you a big rush of adrenaline. It's like being a superhero flying up into the clouds and then swooshing down at lightning speed!

FLYING COASTERS

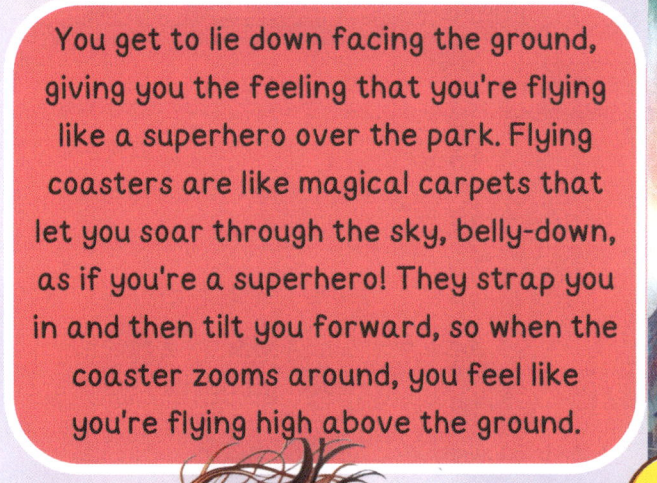

You get to lie down facing the ground, giving you the feeling that you're flying like a superhero over the park. Flying coasters are like magical carpets that let you soar through the sky, belly-down, as if you're a superhero! They strap you in and then tilt you forward, so when the coaster zooms around, you feel like you're flying high above the ground.

OH NO!

People love them because they give you the thrilling sensation. You get to swoop up, down, and all around, just like you're flying for real. It's like having your own wings and zooming through the air, feeling the breeze as you go!

Flying coasters give you the superpower to swoop through the air like a superhero!

Designing Roller Coasters

INTENDED RIDER

When engineers start thinking about making a new roller coaster, they first think about who will ride it. This is really important because it helps them decide how fast it should go, how tall it should be, what kind of track to use, how exciting it should be, what materials to build it with, and what kind of ride it will be.

For families, the ride might be a bit gentler, with fun turns and maybe a few small dips, so everyone can laugh and have fun together.

Little kids would love the coaster to be less scary, with gentle slopes, easy turns, and lots of colorful themes.

WHO WILL RIDE IT?

For teens and adventure seekers: They might make the roller coaster really fast, with big drops and lots of exciting loops because they love thrills! A super-fast coaster might be great for thrill-seekers.

PRE-CONSTRUCTION PLANNING

SPACE AVILABLE

When engineers are planning a new roller coaster, they have to think about the space available. Engineers look at the park and decide where the roller coaster can fit.

They need to calculate the area they have for the coaster so they can design a track that fits perfectly without being too squished or too spread out.

BUDGET FOR BUILDING

Engineers have a certain amount of money they can spend to build the coaster. They have to think carefully about how much everything costs, from the nails and screws to the big steel beams. They want to make sure they can afford to build something really fun and safe without spending too much money.

ROLLER COASTER LAYOUT

A roller coaster layout is like a big, twisty map that shows where the roller coaster goes. It's like the path your toy train takes but for roller coasters! Engineers design this layout to make sure the ride is super fun, totally safe, and works just right.

SAFETY FIRST — HAVE FUN

The most important thing is to keep everyone safe while they're having fun.

The engineers plan the roller coaster path very carefully so that it's strong, stable, and won't go too fast or slow. They want to make sure you scream with excitement and laugh a lot! They design loops, drops, and turns that are thrilling and make the ride super enjoyable.

JUST HAVE FUN

PARTS OF THE ROLLER

Loops Going Upside Down

Loops are the circles that turn you upside down! They're super fun and give you that funny feeling in your tummy. When you reach the top of the loop on a roller coaster, you're flipped all the way upside down! It feels like you're floating for a bit, and you get to see everything as if you were hanging from the ceiling – the whole world turns topsy-turvy!

Turns and Twists

Whirling Around

These are the parts where the coaster curves around, sometimes gently and sometimes really sharply, so you feel like you're zipping around super fast!

Corkscrews Spiraling Fun

Think of a roller coaster track that twists around like a twisty slide or a spiral staircase. It spins the train in circles while it moves along, just like twisting a wet towel really tight. It's a fun part of the ride where you get to whirl around and around!

figure-eight
Looping in Style

Imagine riding a roller coaster and suddenly, the track makes a shape like the number 8! It's called a figure-eight. When you ride through it, you go around and around, feeling like you're looping and twisting in a big, fun circle. It's like going on a wild adventure where you're zooming through twists and turns, feeling the excitement as you go up, down, and all around!

Hills Climbing to the Top

Roller coaster hills are like giant ramps that take you higher and higher. As the coaster climbs, you can see the world getting smaller below you. It's an exciting feeling, like reaching the top of a mountain or flying high in the sky. At the top of the hill, you'll feel like you're on top of the world! The coaster slows down for just a moment, giving you time to take in the view before the real fun begins.

Drops

Plunging into Fun

After you go up, you must come down! Drops are where the coaster comes down fast from a hill, and you feel like you're falling – it's so exciting! The coaster speeds down the hill, and you'll feel like you're flying through the air. It's a rush of adrenaline hold on tight and enjoy the ride! Roller coaster hills and drops are carefully designed by engineers to give riders a thrilling experience. They use math and science to make sure the ride is safe and fun!

Drops and Dips
Up and Down Adventures

In addition to big drops, roller coasters often have smaller drops and dips throughout the ride. These give you little bursts of excitement as you go up and down, like riding over small hills in a car.

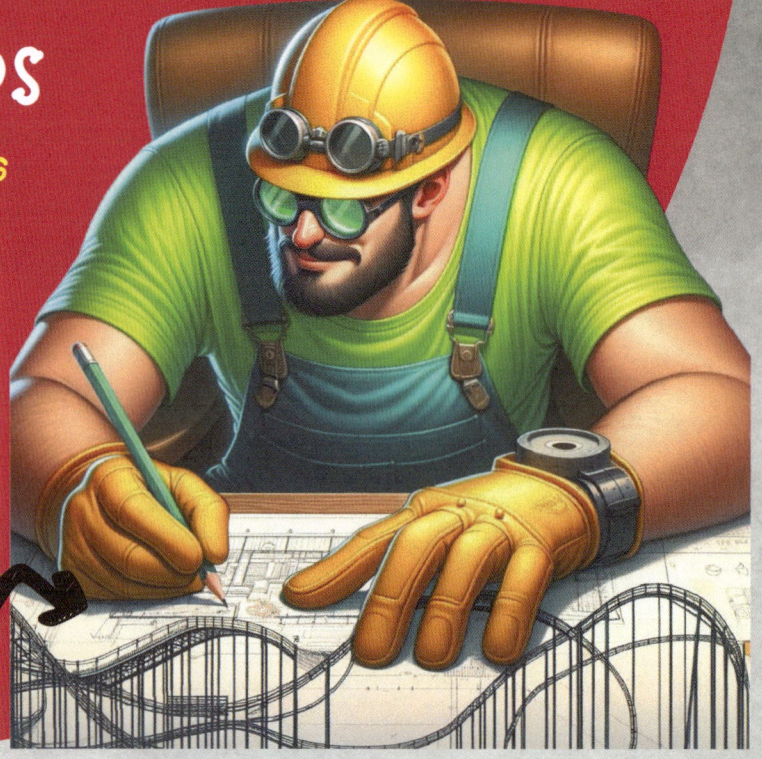

loops, hills and drops are not just for fun

The loops that flip you upside-down, the towering hills that give you butterflies, and the speedy drops that make you shout with joy are all special parts of the ride. But guess what? They're not just there for fun.

They're actually cool ways to explore the laws of a big science called physics! Engineers use lots of math and science to design the coaster track. They carefully design the size, height, and length of the loops, hills, and drops to make sure the roller coaster moves just right, giving you that thrilling ride while keeping everything safe and sound.

NO ENGINE NEEDED

Here's a surprising fact: unlike cars or buses, roller coasters don't have engines. That's right, no motors to power them up or make them go zoom! So, how do they move so fast and far? It's all thanks to a special kind of science magic and some clever design tricks.

Did you know that coasters don't have engines?

It's a secret trick of physics! It is called "energy transfer."

NO ENGINE!

Where does all the coaster energy come from?

Physic's trick

The Mighty lift hill

Where the Adventure Begins

The first big hill on a roller coaster is super tall, like a mountain reaching for the clouds! It's the tallest hill on the whole ride, and it's where the excitement starts to build. It is often called the "lift hill." This is the initial big hill that the coaster climbs right after leaving the station. It's where the coaster gains a lot of its energy.

Lifts Systems

Engineers use many clever methods to get the roller coaster up the first big hill, even without an engine. Here's how they do it:

Lift Hill

How does the roller coaster climb up that huge first hill if it doesn't have an engine to power it up?

1. Chain Lift

Imagine your bike chain, but way bigger! This big chain pulls the roller coaster train up high hills. When you hear that click-click-click sound on the way up, it's this giant chain doing its job!

2. Electromagnetic Launch

Imagine playing with two magnets and trying to stick their south ends together. You've felt how they push each other away, right? That push-away trick is exactly how this roller coaster system works. The track has special magnets, and the coaster has them too. When they line up so the same ends face each other, they repel, or push away, strongly. This push is what makes the coaster zoom off super fast up the lift hill!

Repel

3. Friction Wheel Lift

There are big wheels spinning really fast, lined up along the track where the roller coaster climbs the hill. These aren't just any wheels; they're special because they touch the bottom of the coaster gently. As the coaster starts going up the hill, each spinning wheel gives it a little push. It's like when you're riding your bike uphill, and someone gives you a nudge to help you along. These wheels are perfectly placed so that as soon as one wheel has done its pushing, the next wheel is ready to keep the coaster moving smoothly upward.

POTENTIAL ENERGY

At the start, the roller coaster is pulled up the first big hill (lift hill) by the chain or any other system, sort of like how you might pull your toy car up to the top of a slope.

PULL

This is usually the tallest point of the ride.

Up to the lift hill - Gain and store energy

When a roller coaster is going up the first big hill, it's doing something really special. It's gaining a special type of energy called potential energy. Think of it like this: when someone pulls you back on a swing, lifting you higher and higher, you feel the tension building up. That tension is like stored energy called (potential energy). It's ready and waiting to make you soar through the air!

It is kind of like when you're at the very top of a swing, ready to swoosh back down.

This is the coaster getting ready for the fun part, like taking a deep breath before shouting "weee"

As the coaster climbs higher and higher up the first hill, it's gathering all the energy it needs for the rest of the ride. The higher the coaster goes, the more energy it stores. It's like the coaster is being charged with energy while climbing the hill.

THE COASTER'S SECRET
ENERGY TRANSFER

Once the coaster reaches the top, it is fully charged with stored energy, known as potential energy. Now, it doesn't need the chain anymore. Gravity starts to pull it down the track, similar to being at the top of a playground slide and rushing down.

This means it has gathered all the energy it needs, thanks to its height, and is ready to convert that energy into speed and motion as it races down.

GO!

KINETIC ENERGY

LET'S GO!

All the potential energy that was stored in the coaster starts to turn into another type of energy called kinetic energy, which is a fancy way to say moving energy that makes the coaster speed up. The kinetic energy is what makes the roller coaster zoom along the tracks, especially after the big drops!

Down the lift hill
Stored energy turning into moving energy speeds up the coaster.

UNDERSTANDING MOMENTUM

The roller coaster uses momentum to speed up when going down hills, but do you know what momentum is?

Momentum on a roller coaster is like when you're riding your bike really fast and then you keep moving quickly even when you stop pedaling. Imagine the roller coaster is like your bike; once it starts going down a big hill, it speeds up and has lots of momentum, which means it can keep going fast around the track, up and down hills, and through loops, without needing to be pushed. Just like your bike keeps rolling fast after the big push, the roller coaster uses its momentum to zip through the whole ride!

So, it is just like when you give a marble a little push at the start of a maze and watch it get pulled by gravity, twisting and turning all the way to the end.

The roller coaster is pulled by gravity when it is at the highest point of the lift hill, and then It used momentum to zoom through the entire track!

ENGINEERING CALCULATIONS

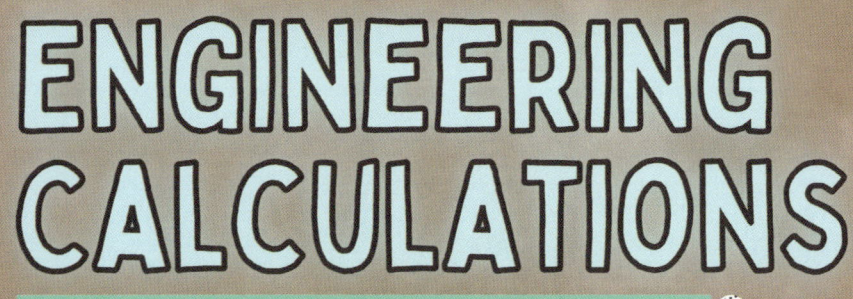

If the lift hill is too short or not long enough, the roller coaster won't have enough momentum to complete the ride and might not be as thrilling.

If the lift hill is too long, the roller coaster could go too fast, making the ride less safe and maybe too scary for the riders.

Making sure the hills and drops are just the right size is important! Engineers do lots of math calculations and use science to calculate the exact size of every hill, drop, and loop to make the ride extra fun and super safe.

Weightlessness In roller coaster

"Weightlessness" is the feeling of having little or no weight. It is as if the force of gravity is canceled out, so there's no force pulling you down, and you might feel like you're floating or drifting. This is what astronauts feel in space. But did you know that you can feel the same sensation on a roller coaster ride? That's what the zero-g roll is all about. Let's learn more about it.

Zero-G Rolls FEELING WEIGHTLESS

A zero G roll is a super cool twisty move in a roller coaster where you feel like you're floating for a moment, just like an astronaut floating in space!

1. GOING UP: START THE ADVENTURE

The track begins by lifting you up, just like climbing a big hill. You feel the excitement building as you go higher and higher.

2. UPSIDE DOWN: TWISTING AND TURNING

At the very top, the track twists, turning you upside down! But don't worry, it's super smooth, like gliding through the air.

3. SPINNING AROUND: FEELING LIKE ASTRONAUTS

As you start to come down, you spin all the way around in a full circle! This is the moment where you feel like you're floating, just like astronauts in space

4. BACK TO NORMAL: RETURNING TO EARTH

After the spin, the track brings you back upright, ready for more fun! It's like coming back down to Earth after an amazing adventure.

The Zero-G Roll combines going up, twisting around, and coming back down to create an awesome feeling of weightlessness. It's a thrilling ride that makes you feel like you're soaring through the sky!

Understanding Roller Coaster
DYNAMICS

There are three awesome forces that make the loops, dips, and speedy turns possible!

Gravity, inertia, and centripetal are three different forces that team up to create the fun and exciting rids.

'Dynamics' is a cool word that engineers use to talk about how these forces work together to make the roller coaster speed up, slow down, and whirl around tracks, making our ride super exciting and fun!

Effect of
1. GRAVITY

Gravity is an invisible force that pulls objects toward the ground.

Imagine you're holding a ball at the top of a hill. If you let it go, it will roll down the hill. Why? Because of gravity! When the coaster climbs to the top of a high track, it is like the ball held high. Once it starts going down the track, gravity pulls it downwards, and the coaster speeds up as it goes lower and lower. This is what makes the roller coaster zoom along the tracks, especially after the big drops!

Effect of
2. Inertia

The exciting feelings on a roller coaster, like your stomach dropping, the feeling of being pushed and pulled and your heart racing, all come from inertia.

Inertia is a fancy word for an object's "laziness."

If something is still, it wants to stay still. If it's moving, it wants to keep moving unless something stops it. This is the inertia law.

Inertia turning the simple movements of the roller coaster into thrilling adventures for the riders

Newton's First Law of Motion.

When the coaster zips down a hill and then races back up, your body wants to keep moving straight down even as the coaster starts to climb. That's why you feel like you're being lifted out of your seat. It's inertia trying to keep you moving in the same direction!

Effect of
3. Centripetal Forces

"Centripetal" means "center-seeking."

This might sound complicated, but it's just about going in circles! Centripetal force is what keeps the roller coaster stuck to the track as it whirls around turns or loops upside down. It also keeps you – pressed against the track so you don't fly off.

Think of spinning a bucket of water in a circle. Why doesn't the water fall out? Because the centripetal force is pushing the water towards the center of the circle, keeping it in the bucket.

So, on a roller coaster, gravity pulls you down the big hills, inertia keeps you moving and gives you those stomach-dropping sensations, and centripetal forces keep you safely in your seat during all the twists and loops. Together, these forces combine to make a roller coaster ride a thrilling mix of speed, spins, and exhilarating fun, all while keeping you safe and sound!

Designing Using Computers

Once engineers have a complete design and finished their forces and sizes calculations, they use special computer programs to design the roller coaster in 3D. This means they create a digital model of the coaster that they can see on the computer screen. In the computer model, engineers can test different designs and make changes easily. They can see if the roller coaster is too steep or if the loops are too tight. They can even simulate what it would feel like to ride the roller coaster!

We can even build a small-scale model of the coaster to test the design and ideas in the real world before creating the full-size version.

Installing the Support Structure

The roller coaster track is held up by a big, strong frame made of steel or wood. It's built to be super sturdy, so it can handle the fast roller coaster and all kinds of weather.

The design of the frame makes sure the ride is fun, safe, and feels exciting, kind of like building a tall, strong tower.

Building the Support Structure is like putting together a huge puzzle, starting with a solid base made by digging holes and filling them with concrete, or using wooden poles if the ground is sandy.

Big machines called cranes help lift and put together the parts of the frame, starting from the bottom and working up to the top.

INSTALLING THE TRACK

Once the big, strong frame is up, it's time to put the tracks on top. After the tracks are all set, They add the chain that pulls the coaster up the hill or the special system that launches it fast. They also put in safety stuff like brakes and systems to make sure the coaster doesn't roll back accidentally. It's really important to get everything just right because they want everyone to be safe while having a great time. And guess what? Riding roller coasters is actually really safe!

CHAIRS' COMFORT AND SAFETY

Safety is the number one priority, so the chairs in the coaster cars have strong seatbelts or harnesses. These aren't just any seatbelts; they're made to fit snugly and keep you in place, even when you're upside down or swirling through big loops. There's also a safety bar or restraint that comes down over your shoulders or around your waist to make extra sure you stay seated safely during the entire ride.

Testing Roller Coaster Design

Super! Safe and comfy

Roller coaster cars are like super-fun race cars with cozy seats! They've got soft cushions to keep you comfy, so even when you zoom around fast or whip through twisty turns, you won't feel too bumpy. There's plenty of space to stretch your legs, and the bars that hold you in are soft so they won't squish you, but they'll still make sure you're safe and sound while you're having a blast.

SANDBAGS TEST

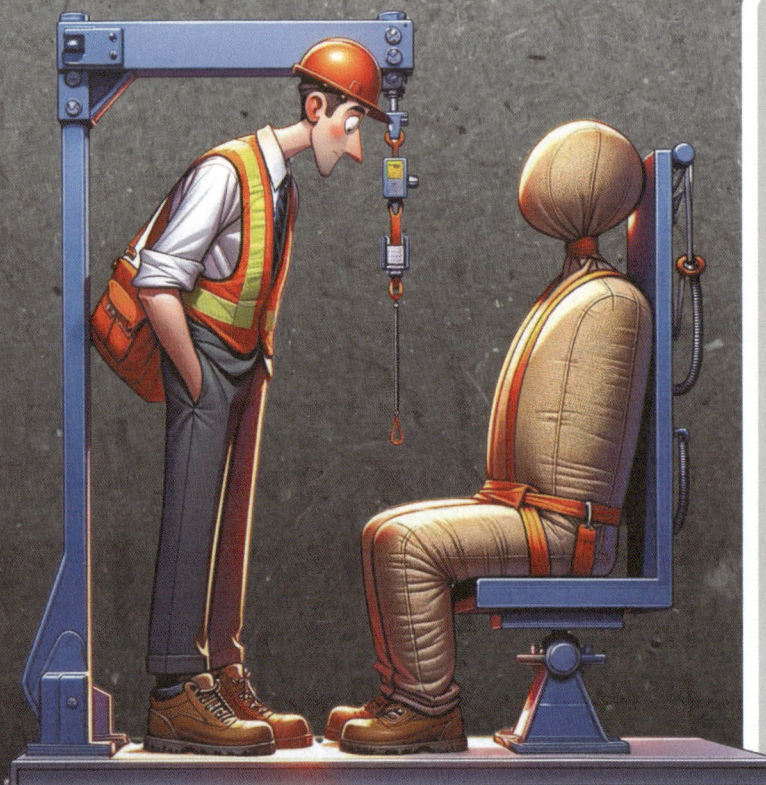

Then, it's time to test the roller coaster to make sure it's perfectly safe. Instead of people, they use sandbags shaped like humans to fill the seats. These sandbags are like pretend passengers that help the engineers see how the roller coaster will work with people on it. They check if the ride is smooth, if it's too fast or slow, and make sure everything is safe and fun.

ROLLER COASTER TEST RUNS

They run the roller coaster with these sandbags over and over, watching closely to see how it goes. They also make sure all the safety signs are in place and that everything looks good, like adding the final touches to make it look cool and fit the theme of the ride. Once everything is checked and double-checked, and the roller coaster passes all the tests, it's ready for people to come and enjoy the exciting ride, knowing they're safe and secure!

Control Room Behind the Scenes

There is a control Room. It is the command center of the roller coaster! Operators here have a super important job, monitoring and controlling the ride. They use big panels with buttons, screens, and switches to keep an eye on everything. They can start or stop the ride, check the speed, and make sure everyone is safe.

MAINTENANCE

Maintenance crews are the unsung heroes who work behind the scenes. Every day, before anyone gets on the ride, these experts check the tracks, the cars, and all the nuts and bolts. They're like detectives, looking for any tiny thing that needs fixing or adjusting, ensuring the coaster is safe and the ride is as smooth as silk.

Engineering Updates

Engineers are always thinking of ways to use new technology to make coasters faster, safer, and more exciting. They might add new kinds of loops, faster launches, or even virtual reality to make the ride more amazing.

Printed in Great Britain
by Amazon